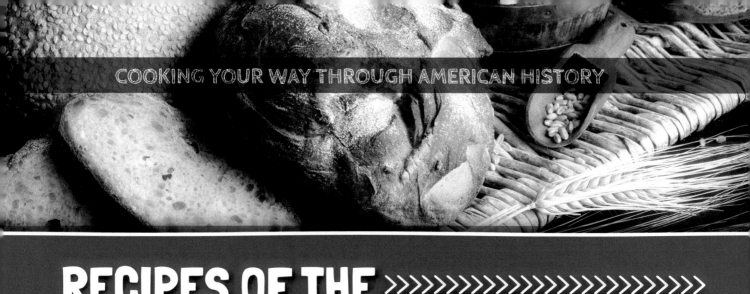

COOKING YOUR WAY THROUGH AMERICAN HISTORY

RECIPES OF THE >>>>>>>>>>>>>>>>>>>>>>
THIRTEEN COLONIES

Joyce Jeffries

KidHaven
PUBLISHING

Published in 2017 by
KidHaven Publishing, an Imprint of Greenhaven Publishing, LLC
353 3rd Avenue
Suite 255
New York, NY 10010

Designer: Deanna Paternostro
Editor: Jennifer Lombardo

Photo credits: Cover, p.1 (top) symbiot/Shutterstock.com; cover, p. 1 (bottom) MPI/Archive Photos/Getty Images; pp. 2, 3, 9, 11, 15, 17, 19, 22, 23, 24 (wood texture) Maya Kruchankova/Shutterstock.com; p. 5 Leonard Zhukovsky/ Shutterstock.com; p. 7 Morphart Creation/Shutterstock.com; pp. 9, 11, 15, 17, 19 (notebook) BrAt82/Shutterstock.com; p. 9 carpe89/Shutterstock.com; p. 10 D Pimborough/Shutterstock.com; p. 11 Cozy Home/Shutterstock.com; p. 13 stockcreations/Shutterstock.com; p. 14 iuliia_n/Shutterstock.com; Nataliya Arzamasova/Shutterstock.com; p. 16 Fotoluminate LLC/Shutterstock.com; p. 17 Lilyana Vynogradova/Shutterstock.com; pp. 19, 21 Brent Hofacker/ Shutterstock.com.

Cataloging-in-Publication Data

Names: Jeffries, Joyce.
Title: Recipes of the thirteen colonies / Joyce Jeffries.
Description: New York : KidHaven Publishing, 2017. | Series: Cooking your way through American history| Includes index.
Identifiers: ISBN 9781534521087 (pbk.) | ISBN 9781534521100 (library bound) | ISBN 9781534521094 (6 pack) | ISBN 9781534521117 (ebook)
Subjects: LCSH: Cooking, American–History–Juvenile literature. | Food habits–United States–History–17th century– Juvenile literature. | Food habits–United States–History–18th century–Juvenile literature. | United States–History–Colonial period, ca. 1600-1775–Juvenile literature.
Classification: LCC TX715.J44 2017 | DDC 641.5973'09032–dc23

Printed in the United States of America

CPSIA compliance information: Batch #CW17KL: For further information contact Greenhaven Publishing LLC, New York, New York at 1-844-317-7404.

Please visit our website, www.greenhavenpublishing.com. For a free color catalog of all our high-quality books, call toll free 1-844-317-7404 or fax 1-844-317-7405.

CONTENTS

Not the United States Yet	4
Bringing New Foods to North America	6
Ways of Cooking	8
Making Up Recipes	10
The Northern Colonies	12
The Middle Colonies	14
The Southern Colonies	16
African Food	18
A Mix of Old and New	20
Glossary	22
For More Information	23
Index	24

NOT THE UNITED STATES YET

In the mid-1600s, groups of people started leaving England and coming to North America. These settlers wanted to make new lives for themselves in a new country. They claimed the land along the East Coast of North America for England and pushed aside the Native Americans who already lived there. Once settled, they were called colonists. The colonies were under British rule, but people came from all over Europe to settle there.

The northern colonies were called New England. They were Massachusetts, New Hampshire, Connecticut, and Rhode Island. The middle colonies, which were along the middle of the East Coast, were New York, New Jersey, Pennsylvania, and Delaware. The southern colonies were North Carolina, South Carolina, Georgia, Virginia, and Maryland. They didn't become the United States until more than 150 years after the first settlers arrived.

The flag of the United States has 50 stars—one for each state—and 13 stripes—one for each of the original colonies.

BRINGING NEW FOODS TO NORTH AMERICA

When the colonists arrived in what's now the United States, they found out that many of the foods they liked to eat weren't native to North America. Apples, wheat, peas, potatoes, and other foods had to be **transported** from European countries. However, the Wampanoag people, a Native American group that was already living there, showed the colonists how to grow foods such as corn, beans, and squash, and how to hunt animals such as geese and elk.

Johanna was a nine-year-old colonial girl in 1720. Her family lived on a farm in New York. They grew corn and kept some cows, goats, chickens, and pigs. The meals Johanna and her family ate were a mix of **traditional** European foods and new North American foods. They made cheese and butter themselves from the milk the cows and goats gave.

Colonists who owned cows would put milk into a butter churn and use a wooden stick, which was called a dasher, to mix the milk until it turned into butter.

WAYS OF COOKING

When the colonists came to North America, they didn't have many of the things we do today. They didn't have ovens in their kitchens for many years. The women did all the cooking by hanging a big iron kettle over the fireplace. Most meals were stews made of meat, corn, turnips, and other vegetables. Johanna's favorite breakfast food was called **hasty** pudding. It was named that because it was quick and easy to make.

Later, ovens were made out of bricks and stones. The women would heat the oven with coals from the fireplace. When it was hot, they would scrape the coals out. Then they would put in breads, pies, or meats with a long, flat shovel called a peel so they wouldn't burn themselves. There were no timers on these ovens and no way to tell how hot they were. The women had to guess whether or not the food was done. Baking this way was hard work, so it was only done once a week.

hasty pudding

Ingredients:
1 cup **cornmeal**
½ teaspoon salt
4 cups water
maple syrup
milk or half-and-half
½ cup raisins (optional)

Directions:
- Mix one cup of water with the cornmeal in a small bowl. You can add raisins if you like.
- Boil the other 3 cups of water with the salt in a medium-size pot.
- When the water boils, turn the heat down to low, and slowly stir in the cornmeal mixture. Stir until the cornmeal is thick, about three to five minutes.
- Turn off the stove, put the lid on the pot, and let it sit for three minutes.
- Stir the pudding again, and serve. Pour the maple syrup or half-and-half over the top.

This serves four people.

Hasty pudding was quick and easy to make, even without a stove or an oven.

MAKING UP RECIPES

Colonial cooks had no cookbooks. Johanna's mother passed on her recipes by teaching them to Johanna. The first American cookbook was published in 1796. One popular recipe at that time was for flat jacks, which are like pancakes. However, they weren't as sweet as the pancakes we eat today because the colonists didn't use sugar. Sugar was shipped from England because it didn't grow in the colonies, but it was too expensive to use every day.

Instead of sugar, most colonists cooked with **molasses** or maple syrup. Molasses also came from English sugar factories, but it was cheaper than sugar. People who lived in the northern colonies made maple syrup from the sap drained from maple trees that grew on their land.

molasses

flat jacks

Ingredients:

1 cup cornmeal
½ cup all-purpose flour
½ teaspoon salt
½ teaspoon baking soda
¼ teaspoon powdered ginger
2 tablespoons butter
1 ½ teaspoons molasses
1 ½ cups buttermilk
¼ cup vegetable oil

Directions:

- Sift the cornmeal, flour, salt, baking powder, and ginger into a medium-size bowl.
- Melt the butter on very low heat in a small pan. Pour the melted butter into another bowl, and mix it with the molasses and buttermilk.
- Stir the liquid mixture into the dry ingredients. Mix until just combined.
- Heat oil in a frying pan.
- Fry about ½ cup of batter at a time.
- Serve with honey or maple syrup.

This serves three people.

This colonial version of pancakes uses molasses as a sweetener instead of sugar.

THE NORTHERN COLONIES

The foods the colonists ate depended on where they lived. It was difficult and expensive to transport food items over long distances, so people had to eat what was nearby. In the northern colonies, this included a lot of seafood and **shellfish** such as cod, tuna, flounder, lobster, crabs, and mussels. It was hard for farmers in the New England colonies to grow enough fruits and vegetables to feed their families, so the colonists hunted in the forests for animals such as deer, geese, swans, rabbits, and bears.

Supply ships were sent from England with things the colonists couldn't get in North America. This included pigs, cows, and goats so the New England colonists could have pork, butter, cheese, and milk to use in their cooking. They generally didn't drink milk because the colonists couldn't keep it fresh without refrigerators.

Mussels were an important food in colonial New England and are still popular today all over the country.

THE MIDDLE COLONIES

Farming was common in the middle colonies. The growing season was longer, and the soil was better than in New England. Many of the colonists in the middle colonies were Dutch and German. They brought their own food traditions with them. Dutch cheeses, cookies, cakes, and pastries became common. Johanna's family was from Germany. Her mother taught her how to make foods such as sauerkraut, pork sausage, and rye bread.

sauerkraut and pork sausage

In Europe, everyone drank beer because the water wasn't good to drink. The water in some parts of North America was good to drink, but the colonists still liked beer better. However, they couldn't make their own beer until the Dutch and the Germans brought wheat and rye with them and started growing them in the middle colonies.

Dutch walnut-cinnamon squares

Ingredients:

8 ounces (1 cup) butter, softened
1 cup sugar
1 egg, separated (the yolk in one bowl,
the egg white in another)
2 cups all-purpose flour
1 teaspoon salt
1 ½ teaspoons cinnamon
1 ½ cups chopped walnuts

Directions:

- Preheat the oven to 325° Fahrenheit (F).
  Grease a 9x13-inch baking pan with
  butter or shortening.
- Cream butter and sugar with a mixer on medium speed for
  two minutes. Stir in egg yolk.
- Sift flour, salt, and cinnamon into a bowl. Add the flour
  mixture to the butter mixture one spoonful at a time, mixing
  at a low speed until dough is formed.
- Press the dough evenly into the pan.
- Beat the egg white in a small bowl with a fork until foamy.
  Pour it over the dough, and spread evenly. Sprinkle the nuts
  onto the dough.
- Bake for 20 to 25 minutes.
- When the pastry is cool, cut it into squares.

This serves four people.

The colonists could find walnuts growing in the woods, so they were popular in colonial dishes.

THE SOUTHERN COLONIES

The southern colonies had big farms called **plantations**. They grew crops such as tobacco, cotton, and rice. The South had a long growing season and a good **climate** for growing these crops, which were called cash crops because they would be sold to many other people in the other colonies, which earned the plantation owners a lot of money. Southerners who didn't live on plantations had smaller farms, where they grew food such as corn, beans, peas, and carrots.

Corn was one food that grew well in all of the colonies. Native Americans taught the colonists how to make corn even more **nutritious** by removing the **hulls** from the **kernels**. They called this corn hominy. The hominy could be cooked with water or milk to make grits, which became a very popular southern breakfast food.

cotton plantation

southern succotash

Ingredients:

2 cups frozen lima beans
2 cups hominy or frozen corn
1 tablespoon butter
½ teaspoon sugar
½ teaspoon salt
¼ teaspoon ground black pepper
¼ cup heavy cream

Directions:

- Cook the lima beans in boiling water in a medium-size pot until nearly soft, and then drain them.
- Put the lima beans back in the pot. Add the corn, butter, sugar, salt, and black pepper. Turn the heat to medium, and put the uncovered pot on the stove. Cook for 10 minutes, stirring every few minutes.
- Turn the heat to low. Stir in the cream, cook for five more minutes, and serve.

This serves four to five people.

Cooking is easier and quicker today than it was for the colonists because of inventions such as stoves, refrigerators, and frozen vegetables.

AFRICAN FOOD

Because plantations were so large, it was impossible for one farmer to do all the work. Plantation owners wanted to save money, so they used slaves for most of the work. Slaves were people who were brought from Africa against their will to work without pay. They had a very hard life. They were forced to work long hours with little rest, and they could be beaten if they worked too slowly or tried to run away. They had no freedom or rights until 1865, when slavery was outlawed.

Although slaves didn't choose to come to what is now the United States, they added a lot to North American food and cooking traditions. Slave owners brought seeds of African plants along with the slaves. These included black-eyed peas, okra, and peanuts. The slaves used these foods to cook meals for themselves. Sometimes they combined foods from Africa and North America to make new dishes.

hoppin' John

Ingredients:
2 cups frozen black-eyed peas
1 medium chopped onion
½ teaspoon salt
½ teaspoon ground black pepper
¼ teaspoon chili powder
1 clove garlic, **minced**
1 bay leaf
8 ounces uncooked bacon

Directions:
- Add the frozen black-eyed peas and one cup of water to a medium-size pot. Turn the heat to medium, and put the pot on the stove.
- While the peas are cooking, add the onion, salt, black pepper, chili powder, garlic, bay leaf, and uncooked bacon.
- When the water boils, turn the heat down to low, cover the pot, and simmer for one hour.
- Stir from time to time. Check to make sure there's some water left in the pot. If it's dry, add 2 tablespoons of water.
- Serve with rice.

This serves two to three people.

Slaves made this dish when they lived on plantations, but it's still very popular all over the southern United States today.

A MIX OF OLD AND NEW

The foods we eat today come from many different places. Colonists such as Johanna and her family created new dishes by mixing their traditional foods with what was available in North America. African slaves weren't considered colonists, but their food became an important part of North American recipes. Native Americans weren't colonists either, because they were already living in North America before the settlers arrived. Without their help, the colonists wouldn't have known what to eat.

This mixing of foods still happens today. Every time a new group of people moves to the United States, they bring their food, spices, and ways of cooking with them. Foods such as nachos, fortune cookies, and pepperoni pizza aren't traditional foods in other countries; they were created when people combined American and traditional foods. Who knows what new, delicious foods will be made next?

Pizza was invented in Italy, but only Americans put pepperoni on it.

GLOSSARY

climate: The usual weather conditions in a particular place or region.

cornmeal: A coarse flour made from crushed corn.

hasty: Done or made very quickly.

hulls: The tips of kernels or seeds.

kernels: Whole grains or seeds of a cereal, such as wheat or corn.

minced: Cut into very small pieces.

molasses: A thick, brown, sweet liquid that is made from raw sugar.

nutritious: Containing anything that a living thing needs for energy, to grow, or to heal.

plantations: Large areas of land, especially in a hot part of the world where crops are grown.

shellfish: An animal, such as a crab or an oyster, that lives in water and has a hard outer shell.

traditional: Having to do with the ways of doing things in a culture that are passed down from parents to children.

transported: To move someone or something from one place to another.

FOR MORE INFORMATION

WEBSITES

History is Served
recipes.history.org/recipeindex
Colonial Williamsburg presents a list of recipes. Each entry on the list first gives the recipe from the original cookbook, then an interpretation that makes it easier for modern cooks.

Interactive History
www.pbs.org/wnet/colonialhouse/history/panoramas.html
Take interactive "tours" of colonial houses, choose the clothes a colonial woman might wear, "translate" 17th-century speech into modern speech, listen to views of life in the colonies, and more!

Mount Vernon Recipes
www.mountvernon.org/recipes
George Washington's home, Mount Vernon, is a museum today. The museum staff created a list of recipes George and Martha Washington might have served to dinner guests.

BOOKS

Garstecki, Julia. *Life in Colonial America*. Minneapolis, MN: Core Library, 2015.

Rissman, Rebecca. *Slavery in the United States*. Minneapolis, MN: ABDO Publishing Company, 2015.

Spilsbury, Louise. *Horrible Jobs in Colonial Times*. New York, NY: Gareth Stevens Publishing, 2014.

INDEX

B
butter, 6, 7, 11, 12, 15, 17

C
cheese, 6, 12, 14
corn, 6, 8, 9, 11, 16, 17
crops, 16

D
drinks, 12, 14

E
England, 4, 10, 12

F
farm, 6, 12, 14, 16, 18
fireplace, 8
fruit, 12

H
hunt, 6, 12

K
kettle, 8

M
meals, 6, 8, 18
meat, 8
molasses, 10, 11

N
Native Americans, 4, 6, 16, 20
North America, 4, 6, 8, 12, 14, 18, 20

P
plantation, 16, 18, 19

R
refrigerator, 12, 17

S
seeds, 18

settlers, 4, 20
slave, 18, 19, 20
sugar, 10, 11, 15, 17

U
United States, 4, 5, 6, 18, 19, 20

V
vegetables, 8, 12, 17

W
Wampanoag, 6